# Contents

# Chapter 1

# All About Plants

Look at this beautiful field of bright sunflowers.
This book will tell you all about them!

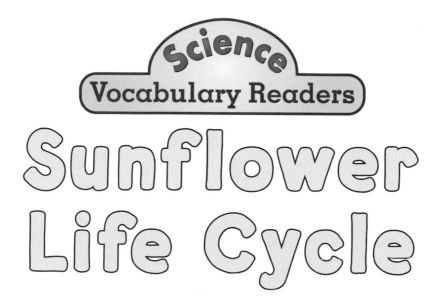

# Science
## Vocabulary Readers
# Sunflower Life Cycle

**Jeff Bauer**

## SCHOLASTIC INC.

NEW YORK • TORONTO • LONDON • AUCKLAND • SYDNEY
MEXICO CITY • NEW DELHI • HONG KONG • BUENOS AIRES

ISBN-13: 978-0-439-87654-4 / ISBN-10: 0-439-87654-0

Photos Credits:
Cover: © Chris Cheadle/Getty Images; title page: © Getty Images; contents page, from top: © Ariel Skelley/Corbis, © Jim Sugar/Corbis, © Getty Images, © Getty Images; page 4: © Ariel Skelley/Corbis; page 5: © Michael Boys/Corbis; page 6: © Rolf Nussbaumer/Nature Picture Library; page 7, left: © Corbis; page 7, right: © Getty; page 8, top right: © Gavin Hellier/Nature Picture Library; page 8, bottom left: © Corbis; page 8, bottom right: © Getty Images; page 9, top left: © Getty Images; page 9, top right: © Corbis; page 9, bottom left: © Getty Images; page 9, bottom right: © Jim Brandenburg/Minden Pictures; page 10: © Jim Sugar/Corbis; page 11: © Getty Images; page 12: © Getty Images; page 13, left: © Bruce Coleman USA Inc.; page 13, right: © National Geographic/Getty Images; page 14: © Getty Images; page 15: © Getty Images; page 16, both: © Getty Images; page 17: © Bilderberg/Peter Arnold Inc.; page 17, inset: © Wim Weenink/Foto Natura/Minden; page 18, left: © Jim Sugar/Corbis; page 18, right: © Getty Images; page 19, left: © Getty Images; page 19, right: © Corbis; page 20: © Getty Images; page 21, left: © Tim Ridley/Getty Images; page 21, right: © TH Foto-Werbung/Science Photo Library; page 22: © Getty Images; page 24: © Manchan/Getty Images; back cover: © Jim Sugar/Corbis.

Photo research by Dwayne Howard
Design by Holly Grundon

Copyright © 2007 by Lefty's Editorial Services
All rights reserved. Published by Scholastic Inc.

12 11                                                        12/0

Printed in the U.S.A.        40
First printing, March 2007

**Fast Fact**

**Plants grow all over the world.**

Sunflowers are plants. So is everything in this garden.

**A hummingbird visits a sunflower.**

Plants are living things. But they do not move around like animals. Plants stay in one place and grow.

**A butterfly drinks nectar.**

**A child eats watermelon.**

Some plants have flowers. Some plants have vegetables or fruits. Both animals and people depend on plants for food.

Plants need air, sun, soil, and water to grow healthy and strong.

tree

watermelon

pansy

There are millions of kinds of plants in the world. Do you know what makes all of them alike?

**grass**

**wheat**

**cactus**

**sunflower**

They all began as tiny seeds! Let's take a look at the life cycle of a sunflower to see how a plant grows.

# Chapter 2

# Seed to Flower

These are sunflower seeds. They get planted in the spring. Why? They need warmth and rain to grow into flowers.

**Plant Parts**

leaves

stem

roots

Rainwater wets the ground. It softens a seed until it bursts open. Then up grows a baby sunflower with roots, a stem, and little green leaves.

**This is a flower bud.**

The plant gets bigger and bigger. It grows a big bud at the top of its stem. Do you know what that bud will become?

Fast Fact

**It takes a sunflower many days to open all the way up.**

The answer is a bright yellow flower! One by one, the **petals** open. Soon the sunflower will be in full **bloom**.

# Chapter 3

# Flower to Seed

Ta-dah! About two months after the seed was planted, the sunflower is all grown-up. It is now in full bloom.

**A bee sucks up nectar.**

A few days later, the sunflower begins to make a sugary liquid called nectar. Buzz, buzz! Bees stop by for a sweet drink.

**Close Up!**

**Pollen grains look like this close up.**

Sunflowers also make a sticky dust called pollen. When bees fly from flower to flower, they spread the dust around. This causes the sunflowers to make new seeds.

**Fast Fact**

The center of a sunflower is packed with hundreds of seeds.

In fall, sunflowers **shrivel** up and start to die. They drop their seeds, which slide into the ground. The seeds stay buried until spring. Then they grow into new sunflowers!

# Life Cycle Review

**1 Day:**
In spring, a sunflower seed is planted in the ground.

**1 Week:**
A sunflower seed bursts open and a little plant grows.

Can you remember the four main parts of a sunflower's life cycle? Take a look.

**2 Months:**
**A sunflower opens all its bright petals and blooms.**

**4 Months:**
**A shriveling sunflower drops its seeds so that new plants can grow.**

A sunflower's life cycle lasts about four months.

# Chapter 4

# Super Sunflowers!

**Fast Fact**

There are **67 different kinds of sunflowers in the world.**

Sunflowers grow all over. Some grow in gardens and fields. Others grow on special sunflower farms like this.

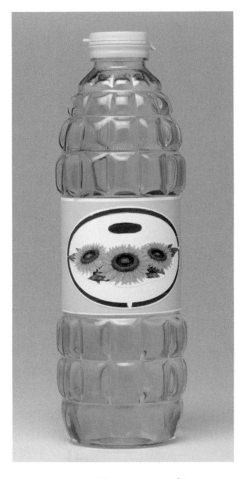

**sunflower oil**          **sunflower seeds**

There are many uses for sunflowers. Oil from sunflowers is used for cooking. You can also eat the seeds. Crunch, crunch, crunch!

You can even pick sunflowers and give them to someone you love. Beautiful!

# Glossary

**bloom** (**bloom**) when a flower opens all the way up

**bud** (**buhd**): a small shoot on a plant that becomes a flower or leaf

**nectar** (**nek**-tur): a sweet liquid that bees and other bugs collect from flowers

**petals** (**pet**-uhlz): one of the colored outer parts of a plant

**pollen** (**pol**-uhn): a sticky dust that plants make; pollen gets spread around, causing plants to make seeds

**roots** (**rootz**): the part of a plant that grows underground; roots hold a plant in place and drink up water

**shrivel** (**shriv**-uhl): to become dry and wrinkled

**stem** (**stem**) the long, main part of a plant from which leaves and flowers grow

# Comprehension Questions

**1.** Can you name four types of plants?

**2.** Can you retell the four main parts of a sunflower's life cycle?

**3.** Can you name two products that come from sunflowers?

**4.** Can you think of four words to describe a sunflower?

## Bonus Fast Facts

- A sunflower can grow to be 18 feet high. That is as tall as a giraffe!

- During the day, every sunflower in a field will turn in the same direction to face the sun.

- Long ago, Native Americans used sunflowers for food.